cooking classics
thailand

cooking classics

thailand

A STEP-BY-STEP COOKBOOK

forest leong

Marshall Cavendish
Cuisine

The publisher wishes to thank Pyrex Metalware, Visions and
Ekco 123 for the loan of kitchen utensils used in this book.

Editors : Lydia Leong, Sylvy Soh
Designer : Lynn Chin Nyuk Ling
Photographer : Jambu Studio

Reprinted 2008, 2009

Published by Marshall Cavendish Cuisine
An imprint of Marshall Cavendish International
1 New Industrial Road, Singapore 536196

Other Marshall Cavendish Offices:
Marshall Cavendish Ltd. 5th Floor, 32-38 Saffron Hill, London EC1N 8FH, UK • Marshall Cavendish
Corporation. 99 White Plains Road, Tarrytown NY 10591-9001, USA • Marshall Cavendish International
(Thailand) Co Ltd. 253 Asoke, 12th Flr, Sukhumvit 21 Road, Klongtoey Nua, Wattana, Bangkok 10110,
Thailand • Marshall Cavendish (Malaysia) Sdn Bhd, Times Subang, Lot 46, Subang Hi-Tech Industrial
Park, Batu Tiga, 40000 Shah Alam, Selangor Darul Ehsan, Malaysia

Marshall Cavendish is a trademark of Times Publishing Limited

National Library Board Singapore Cataloguing in Publication Data

Leong, Forest, 1970
Cooking classics : Thailand / Forest Leong. – Singapore : Marshall Cavendish Cuisine, c2007.
p. cm. – (Cooking classics)
Includes index.
ISBN-13 : 978-981-261-330-1
ISBN-10 : 981-261-330-7

1. Cookery, Thai. I. Title. II. Series: Cooking classics

TX724.5.T5
641.59593 -- dc22   SLS2007016793

Printed in Singapore by Times Printers Pte Ltd

contents

introduction

'Thai cuisine' suggests a collective group of various dishes that are synonymous with Thailand's culture. To the common person who might enjoy Thai food on a few occasions, images such as the ubiquitous Tom Yum Prawns *(Tom Yum Goong)*, Stir-fried Thai Noodles *(Pad Thai)* and green curry are conjured up in one's mind. However, such a generalisation would be rank injustice to Thai cuisine, especially when it is so deeply entrenched in the way of Thai people, their culture and their philosophy. Thai cuisine is a medley of flavours, ranging from hot and spicy, sweet and savoury to sour; the intricacy of its cuisine lies in the way each of these tastes come together in the unlikeliest of manners.

Savouring Thai food can occur in a variety of ways; for instance, indulging your senses by sampling the teeming potpourri of Thai street food along a crowded street in Bangkok, or sitting down to a simple, home-cooked meal in a typical Thai home. Thai people view eating as an integral aspect of life; they enjoy their food spontaneously and welcome foreigners to do the same.

Central Thailand cuisine has the widest array of flavours: spicy, sour, sweet and salty. Whether it is a piquant salad laced with a tangy dressing, a steaming bowl of beef noodles, or a smooth, spicy curry laced with coconut milk, there is a great variety to choose from. As central Thailand is comparatively modern and cosmopolitan in contrast to the rest of Thailand, different aspects of world cuisines have crept in, resulting in easy availability of fusion-styled dishes. Due to a majority of Muslims living in the south, cuisine from the southern part of Thailand has Malay and Indian influences. Food is exceedingly spicy, rich and intense in flavour, cooked with an array of herbs and spices that are not commonly found in other parts of Thailand. Southern Thailand cuisine also has the widest variety of seafood dishes.

Northern Thailand cuisine tends to be milder, preferring light, refreshing salads and salty tastes to sweet and sour. Steamed glutinous rice is served as the main staple as compared to the central and southern regions, which serve jasmine rice. It is hard to find seafood dishes, due to the North's remote location from the sea, so red meat and poultry tend to be the order of the day. Northeastern dishes are largely influenced by Laotian cuisine; the locals prefer to prepare their food fried, with spicy, ground meats and shredded vegetable salads.

Thankfully, one need not neccessarily look to travelling all the way to Thailand to sample its cuisine nowadays. Almost every country in Asia and beyond has at least one local Thai eatery in the neighbourhood. Like its people and their intricate culture, Thai food has become one of the world's most favoured and well-received cuisines.

Thai cooking techniques typically consist of steaming, boiling, simmering, grilling, stir-frying and deep-frying.

cooking techniques

boiling and simmering

As one of the easiest cooking techniques, boiling is employed in Thai cooking when making stock out of meat bones or vegetables, and certain soups, stews and curries. There are many advantages to boiling; bacteria that is usually present in raw food is quickly killed, thus rendering the food safe for consumption. When making soup stock, much flavour from the boiled ingredients is retained as well, making the stock tasty and nutritious. Simmering implies bringing food to a slow boil over low heat. It a preferred method for making gravies, stews and curries. Tough cuts of meat can also be tenderised in the cooking process. Always be careful not to overboil, as this will result in a loss of vitamins and flavour for certain foods.

grilling

Grilling is a traditional Thai technique of cooking poultry, red meat and seafood. Grilling can refer to two methods: the first scenario involves food being cooked over a dry source of heat, which is typically over a barbecue pit or roasting spit. The second method involves food being cooked under a dry source of heat, such as in an oven. By allowing the food to cook in its own natural juices, grilling is a healthy alternative to deep-frying. Although Thai people traditionally grilled their food over a charcoal fire, many now prefer to use conventional ovens due to the convenience of preparation work.

steaming

Steaming involves cooking food that is raised over boiling liquid in a wok, or heavy pot with a lid. The food is cooked from the rising vapour of the boiling liquid. Steaming helps to retain most of the food item's natural nutrients as it does not come into direct contact with the boiling liquid. Like the Chinese, Thais usually steam their fish and seafood dishes and certain desserts.

stir-frying

A quick and simple cooking method, stir-frying was introduced into Thai cooking in ancient times, when Chinese settlers moved from the mainland to Siam (the ancient name for Thailand). Stir-frying involves heating oil in a wok or frying pan, and using a spatula to stir or toss ingredients in a quick, consistent motion. It is advisable to cook tougher cuts of meat or vegetables with hard textures, such as carrots and potatoes, in the initial stage of stir-frying a dish with mixed ingredients, as they might need more time to cook thoroughly.

salads

Salads are a typical component of northern and northeastern Thai cuisine. The method of preparation varies from the type of ingredients used in the salad, according to whether the salad is meat or vegetable-based. Most Thai salads involve chopping or slicing fresh, crisp vegetables and fruit, combining them together and mixing them with a specially prepared sauce. Freshly-picked herbs and spices are also a common feature in Thai salads; to release flavour, herbs such as basil, mint and coriander (cilantro) are often bruised or coarsely chopped before mixing them in with the rest of the salad. Meat-based salads require the meat to be par-cooked prior to combining with other salad ingredients.

sauces

Whether as a salad dressing or condiment, sauces are a ubiquitous feature in Thai meals. A dipping sauce, for instance, is usually prepared by pounding ingredients together with a mortar and pestle before combining with a readymade paste or seasoning. The simplest dipping sauce involves chopping a handful of bird's eye chillies and putting them into a small saucer of fish sauce. More elaborate dips involve frying or preserving the ingredients before they can be used as a dip.

vegetables and salads

pomelo salad 18

green mango salad 21

beef salad with grapes 22

glass noodle salad 25

tempura vegetables with prawn paste dip 26

grilled pork salad 29

betel leaf wrapped snack 30

seafood salad 33

pomelo salad yum som-o

Sweet, juicy pomelo with crushed peanuts and refreshing herbs make for a perfect salad on a hot day. Serves 4

Grated skinned coconut 2 Tbsp

Dried prawns (shrimp) 1 Tbsp, washed and drained

Pomelo 1, small

Prawns (shrimp) 100 g (3¹/₂ oz), boiled and peeled

Chicken breast 100 g (3¹/₂ oz), boiled and shredded

Crisp-fried shallots 1 Tbsp

Crisp-fried garlic 1 Tbsp

Unsalted roasted peanuts a handful, crushed

Shallot 1, finely sliced

Red chillies 2, seeded and finely sliced into strips

Mint leaves 1 sprig

Dressing

Lime juice 1 Tbsp

Thai tom yum paste 1 Tbsp

Salt ¹/₂ tsp

Sugar 1 tsp

1 Heat a saucepan for frying over medium heat and dry-fry grated coconut until fragrant and golden brown in colour. Remove from heat and pour into a mixing bowl.

2 Place dried prawns into a blender (food processor) and blend until prawns are light and fluffy in texture. Set aside.

3 Halve pomelo, and separate segments. Remove pips and discard membrane.

4 Add the pomelo sacs, prawns, shredded chicken, crisp-fried shallots and garlic, peanuts. sliced shallots and red chilli strips to grated coconut in mixing bowl and toss lightly.

5 In a separate mixing bowl, combine the dressing ingredients and mix well until sugar dissolves. Pour the dressing over salad ingredients and toss lightly again.

6 Serve garnished with mint leaves.

green mango salad yum ma-maung

A popular dish in Northern Thailand, this lightly spicy, tangy salad stimulates an appetite for the main course. Serves 4

Dried prawns (shrimp) 2 Tbsp, washed and drained

Green mango 1

Carrot 1, peeled and finely sliced into strips

Shallots 2, peeled and finely sliced

Unsalted roasted peanuts a handful

Coriander (cilantro) leaves 1 sprig

Dressing

Bird's eye chillies 2, finely chopped

Fish sauce 1 Tbsp

Sugar 1 Tbsp

1 Place dried prawns (shrimp) in a blender (food processor) and blend until prawns are light and fluffy in texture. Pour into a mixing bowl and set aside.

2 Peel green mango and cut into thin strips approximately measuring 5-cm (2-in) long. Soak mango strips in cold water for a few minutes to crisp them, then drain.

3 Combine dressing ingredients and mix well until sugar dissolves.

4 Add mango strips, carrot strips, shallots, peanuts and dressing to the blended dried prawns. Toss lightly until well mixed.

5 Serve garnished with coriander leaves.

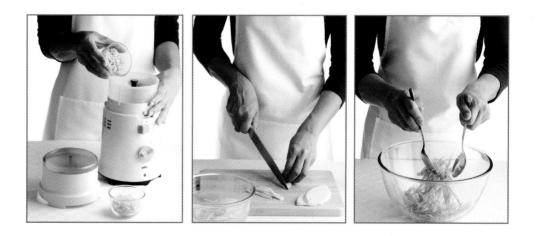

beef salad with grapes
yum nuea yang ar-ngoong

Delicately seared tenderloin and tangy grapes come together to produce a unique Thai meat salad with a modern twist. **Serves 4**

Beef tenderloin 400 g (14^1/$_3$ oz), cut into 1-cm (^{1}/$_2$-in) thick slices

Red and green grapes 70 g (2^1/$_2$ oz), halved and seeded

Shallots 2, peeled and finely sliced

Spring onion (scallion) 1, cut into 2.5-cm (1-in) lengths

Kaffir lime leaves 2–3, finely sliced

Mint leaves a handful

Dressing

Garlic 2 cloves, peeled and finely chopped

Galangal 2.5-cm (1-in) knob, peeled and finely chopped

Mint leaves a handful

Red chilli 1, finely sliced

Lime juice 60 ml (2 fl oz / ^{1}/$_4$ cup)

Fish sauce 1–2 Tbsp

Sugar 1 tsp

1   Heat a pan over high heat. Sear beef tenderloin for 5–7 minutes, until meat is cooked and nicely browned, then remove from heat.

2   Slice beef into strips and set aside.

3   To make the dressing, blend (process) garlic, galangal, mint leaves and red chilies in a blender until finely minced. Add lime juice, fish sauce and sugar and mix well.

4   Toss beef tenderloin slices with dressing, then add grapes and shallots and toss lightly again.

5   Serve garnished with spring onion, kaffir lime leaves and mint leaves.

glass noodle salad yum woon-sen

A savoury, tangy noodle salad that serves as a light appetiser. Serves 4

Green bean vermicelli 100 g (3$^1/_2$ oz),
soaked to soften and drained

Chicken stock (see page 112) 250 ml
(8 fl oz / 1 cup)

Minced pork 200 g (7 oz)

Prawns (shrimps) 200 g (7 oz), cooked
and peeled

Shallots 2, peeled and finely sliced

Unsalted roasted peanuts a handful

Spring onion (scallion) 1, cut into 2.5-cm
(1-in) lengths

Dressing

Fish sauce 2 Tbsp

Lime juice 60 ml (2 fl oz / $^1/_4$ cup)

Red chilli 1, sliced

Sugar $^1/_2$ tsp

1 Chop the vermicelli into 10–12-cm (4–5-in) lengths.

2 Bring stock to the boil over medium heat and add minced pork. Stir
gently until pork is cooked. Add vermicelli, stirring quickly until
vermicelli turns translucent. Remove from heat, pour into a mixing bowl
and set aside.

3 In a separate mixing bowl, combine the dressing ingredients and mix well
until sugar dissolves. Pour dressing over the vermicelli and toss lightly.

4 Add prawns, shallots, peanuts and spring onions and toss lightly again.
Serve warm.

tempura vegetables with
prawn paste dip num prig-ka-pi

An assortment of fresh and tempura-style vegetables served with a spicy prawn paste concoction. **Serves 4**

Aubergine (eggplant/brinjal) 1, sliced

Carrot 1, peeled and sliced

Cooking oil for deep-frying

Fresh vegetables (long beans, ladies fingers [okra], cabbage)

Tempura batter

Plain (all-purpose) flour 140 g (5 oz)

Sodium bicarbonate 1 tsp

Salt 1/2 tsp

Egg 1, beaten

Vegetable oil 1 Tbsp

Cold water 250 ml (8 fl oz / 1 cup)

Dipping sauce

Bird's eye chillies 2–3, bruised

Red chillies 2, finely chopped

Garlic 10 cloves, peeled

Fish sauce 60 ml (2 fl oz / 1/4 cup)

Dried prawns (shrimps) 1 Tbsp, washed and drained

Lime juice 125 ml (4 fl oz / 1/2 cup)

Palm sugar 1 Tbsp

Prawn (shrimp) paste 2 Tbsp

1 Prepare tempura batter. Place plain flour, sodium bicarbonate and salt in a mixing bowl. Add egg, vegetable oil and water, and whisk well to break up any lumps.

2 Dip aubergine and carrot slices in tempura batter.

3 Heat oil for deep-frying and fry the battered aubergine and carrot slices until light golden brown in colour. Drain well and set aside.

4 Use a mortar and pestle and pound bird's eye chillies, red chillies and garlic into a fine paste. Combine with remaining dipping sauce ingredients in a mixing bowl and mix well.

5 Serve tempura and fresh vegetables with dipping sauce on the side.

grilled pork salad yum kor-moo yaang

The contrast of spicy, piquant sauce with cool strips of cucumber makes a perfectly balanced salad for a light starter. Serves 4

Cucumbers 2

Pork shoulder 500 g (1 lb 1 ¹/₂ oz), finely sliced

Mint leaves a handful

Dressing

Coriander (cilantro) leaves and root 2 sprigs, finely chopped

Fish sauce 2 Tbsp

Garlic 3 cloves, peeled and finely chopped

Lime juice 3 Tbsp

Meat or vegetable stock 2 Tbsp

Red chilli 1, finely chopped

Sugar a pinch

1 Heat a pan over medium heat. Sear pork for 5–7 minutes until meat is cooked and nicely browned, then remove from heat.

2 Peel cucumbers and cut each into 5–7-cm (2–3-in) lengths. Halve each piece and scrape out seeds. Slice into medium-fine strips, and arrange the strips on a shallow plate. Set aside.

3 Place dressing ingredients into a blender (food processor) and blend a fine paste.

4 Arrange pork slices over cucumber strips and spoon dressing over.

5 Serve garnished with mint leaves.

betel leaf wrapped snack miang kum

A traditional Thai snack that satisfies hunger pangs in between meals. It combines the best Thai flavours and textures in a few small bites. **Serves 4**

Betel leaves (or butterhead lettuce) 10

Filling

Bird's eye chillies 3, finely sliced

Ginger 2.5-cm (1-in) knob, peeled and finely diced

Grated coconut 70 g (2^1/$_2$ oz), lightly toasted (see page 18)

Green limes 2, unpeeled and diced

Prawns (shrimps) 70 g (2^1/$_2$ oz), cooked and peeled

Shallot 1, peeled and finely sliced

Toasted dried prawns (shrimps) 2 Tbsp

Unsalted roasted peanuts, a handful

Sauce

Galangal 70 g (2^1/$_2$ oz)

Ginger 2.5-cm (1-in) knob, peeled and finely sliced

Grated coconut 70 g (2^1/$_2$ oz), lightly toasted

Ground dried prawns (shrimp) 70 g (2^1/$_2$ oz) (see page 21)

Shallots 140 g (5 oz), peeled and finely sliced

Prawn (shrimp) paste 1 Tbsp

Palm sugar 140 g (5 oz)

Salt to taste

Water 500 ml (16 fl oz / 2 cups)

Sugar 70 g (2^1/$_2$ oz)

1 Using a paring knife or vegetable peeler, peel galangal, then cut into fine slices.

2 Place sauce ingredients, except for the palm sugar, salt, water and white sugar into a blender (food processor) and blend into a fine paste. Bring paste to the boil over medium heat, then add palm sugar, salt, water and sugar. Stir continuously until sauce thickens to a honey-like consistency.

3 Spoon a small portion of each filling ingredient on the centre of each betel leaf. Drizzle with 1 tsp of sauce and fold edge of leaf over filling. Serve.

seafood salad yum ta-lay

Lightly cooked seafood, laced with a delicately spicy dressing. **Serves 4**

Red chillies 2

Chinese celery 2 stalks

Seafood (prawns [shrimps], squid tubes and mussels) 500 g (1 lb 1 ¹/₂ oz), cleaned

Shallots 3, peeled and finely sliced

Dressing

Bird's eye chilli 1, finely chopped

Fish sauce 1–2 Tbsp

Garlic oil 1 Tbsp

Lime juice 3 Tbsp

Sugar a pinch

1 Wash seafood. Peel prawns, then make a slit down the back of each prawn. Peel and clean squid tubes (see page 80). Slit tubes, cut into large rectangular pieces and score insides with criss-cross cuts.

2 Seed 1 red chilli by making an incision down the length. Use the sharp tip of the knife to remove as many seeds as possible. Finely slice into strips and set aside. Cut remaining chilli into rounds.

3 Pluck leaves from Chinese celery and set aside. Chop stems into 2.5-cm (1-in) lengths.

4 Bring some water to the boil over medium heat. Poach the seafood for 5–7 minutes, or until seafood is cooked. Drain well and set aside.

5 Combine red chilli strips and rounds, Chinese celery stems and dressing ingredients in a mixing bowl and toss lightly. Add seafood and toss lightly again.

6 Serve immediately.

rice and noodles

beef brisket noodles 36

hot basil minced meat with rice 39

fish curry noodles 40

stir-fried thai noodles 43

pineapple rice 44

claypot prawn vermicelli 47

prawn paste rice 48

beef brisket noodles kuay tiew nuea

A warm, flavourful broth with tender beef slices served with crunchy bean sprouts. Serves 4

Vegetable stock (see page 112) 2 litres (3¹/₅ pints / 8 cups)

Beef brisket 1 kg (2 lb 3 oz)

Coriander (cilantro) 2 sprigs, with root bruised

Cinnamon sticks 2

Star anise 3

Pickled garlic (available at Asian supermarkets) 30 g (1 oz)

Rice noodles 300 g (10¹/₂ oz), soaked to soften and drained

Bean sprouts 280 g (10 oz)

Spring onion (scallion) 1, finely chopped

Garlic oil 60 ml (2 fl oz / ¹/₄ cup)

Ground white pepper a pinch

Chinese celery 2 stalks, cut into short lengths

Seasoning

Rock sugar or granulated sugar 1 Tbsp

Fish sauce 125 ml (4 fl oz / ¹/₂ cup)

Dark soy sauce 1 Tbsp

Ground white pepper 1 Tbsp

Dipping sauce

White vinegar 60 ml (2 fl oz / ¹/₄ cup)

Red chillies 2, finely chopped

Garlic 3 cloves, peeled and finely chopped

1 Bring stock to the boil over medium heat. Add beef brisket, coriander, cinnamon sticks, star anise, pickled garlic and seasoning. Return stock to the boil and leave for 10 minutes. Lower heat and simmer until beef is tender. Remove beef from stock and slice. Set beef aside and keep stock warm.

2 Blanch rice noodles in hot water for 5–7 minutes. Drain, then divide noodles among 4 serving bowls. Add beef brisket slices, bean sprouts, spring onion, 1 tsp of garlic oil and pepper. Gently ladle stock over.

3 Combine ingredients for dipping sauce in a small saucer.

4 Serve beef noodles garnished with Chinese celery, and dipping sauce on the side.

hot basil minced meat with rice
kao pad kra-prow moo

The hot basil leaves and bird's eye chillies give this simple dish its
typical Thai flavours. **Serves 4**

Hot basil leaves a few full sprigs

Cooking oil 1 Tbsp

Garlic 5 cloves, peeled and finely chopped

Bird's eye chillies 2–3, finely chopped

Minced pork 300 g (10½ oz)

Hon shimeji mushrooms 30 g (1 oz)

Red chilli 1, finely sliced

Eggs 4

Seasoning

Fish sauce 1 tsp

Oyster sauce 2 tsp

Sugar ½ tsp

1 Pick the smaller hot basil leaves from the sprigs, as they are more
   flavourful. Wash the selected leaves in cold water, drain and set aside.

2 Heat cooking oil for stir-frying over medium heat. Add garlic and bird's
   eye chillies and stir-fry until fragrant.

3 Add pork, hon shimeji mushrooms, seasoning, hot basil leaves and red
   chilli. Continue to stir-fry until pork is cooked. Remove from heat and
   set aside.

4 Heat a pan and grease lightly with oil. Cook eggs sunny-side up.

5 Spoon minced meat onto 4 serving plates and top with white rice.
   Place an egg on top and serve garnished as desired.

fish curry noodles kha nom jean

An authentic southern Thai curry noodle dish that is made fragrant with coconut milk and lemon grass. **Serves 4**

Fish fillet (sea bass or mackerel) 300 g (11 oz)

Water 500 ml (16 fl oz / 2 cups)

Coconut milk 1 litre (1³/₅ pints / 4 cups)

Coconut cream 125 ml (4 fl oz / ¹/₂ cup)

Fish sauce 3 Tbsp

Sugar to taste

Fresh rice vermicelli 600 g (1 lb 5¹/₃ oz)

Hard-boiled eggs 2-3, peeled and cut into quarters

Bitter gourd 70 g (2¹/₂ oz), halved, cored, thinly sliced and blanched

Long beans 70 g (2¹/₂ oz), cut into 12-cm (5-in) lengths and knotted

Bean sprouts 70 g (2¹/₂ oz), tailed and blanched

Hairy basil leaves a handful

Fish curry paste

Dried chillies 5

Galangal 2.5-cm (1-in) knob, peeled and finely chopped

Lesser galangal 140 g (5 oz), peeled and finely chopped

Lemon grass 1 stalk, thinly sliced

Garlic 10 cloves, peeled

Shallots 30 g (1 oz), peeled and sliced

Prawn (shrimp) paste 1 tsp

1 Fillet the fish by using a sharp knife to make an incision along the head and gill plates. Do not cut the head off. Without removing knife, turn the blade in the direction of the tail and run it down the entire length of the body in one smooth motion. Repeat step for the other side of fish. Rinse fillets and pat dry. Set aside.

2 Prepare curry paste. Use a smaller knife to make a medium-length incision down the length of each dried chilli. Use the sharp tip of the knife to pick out as many seeds as possible, then soak seeded chillies in cold water to remove any remaining seeds.

3 Combine all paste ingredients in a blender (food processor) and blend into a fine paste. Transfer to a mixing bowl and set aside.

4 Bring 500 ml (16 fl oz / 2 cups) water to the boil over medium heat and add fish fillets. When fillets are cooked, remove, drain and set aside. Lower heat, leaving fish stock to simmer gently.

5 Add cooked fillets to fish curry paste to marinate lightly. Add both fish and fish paste to simmering fish stock, and gently stir in coconut milk and cream. Season with fish sauce and sugar, then return to the boil before removing from heat.

6 Divide vermicelli, hard-boiled eggs, bitter gourd, long beans, bean sprouts and hairy basil leaves among 4 serving bowls. Ladle fish curry over just before serving.

stir-fried thai noodles pad thai

This healthy version of the ubiquitous Thai fried noodles is full of flavour — just like what one might find at roadside food stalls in Bangkok. **Serves 4**

Cooking oil 2 Tbsp

Firm bean curd 60 g (2¼ oz)

Bean sprouts 280 g (10 oz), tailed

Cooking oil 4 Tbsp

Prawns (shrimps) 100 g (3½ oz), peeled

Chopped dried radish 3 Tbsp

Dried prawns (shrimp) 3 Tbsp

Rice noodles 200 g (7 oz), soaked to soften and drained

Water 2 Tbsp

Ground peanuts 3 Tbsp

Chilli powder ½ tsp

Sugar 1 tsp

Chives 2, cut into 2.5-cm (1-in) lengths

Parsley a handful

Seasoning

Tamarind juice (see page 113) 2 Tbsp

Sugar 2 Tbsp

Fish sauce 1 Tbsp

1 Gently dice bean curd by cutting into 1-cm (½-in) strips, then cutting the strips into cubes.

2 Pick tails off bean sprouts, then rinse and drain well.

3 Heat 2 Tbsp cooking oil in a pan over medium heat. Stir-fry bean curd and prawns until prawns change colour and are cooked. Remove from heat and set aside.

4 Using the same pan, heat remaining 2 Tbsp cooking oil and add dried radish and dried prawns. Stir-fry for 4–5 minutes. Add rice noodles, water, ground peanuts, seasoning and stir-fry until noodles for 5–7 minutes. Add the bean curd, prawns, bean sprouts and chives and continue to stir-fry for another 4-5 minutes.

5 Serve with raw bean sprouts, fresh lime quarters, chilli powder and sugar on the side.

pineapple rice kao pad sap-pa-rod

This simple and quick rice dish is made sweet and lightly spicy with the tantalising combination of juicy tropical pineapple, curry paste and red chilli. **Serves 4**

Pineapple 1, medium

Chinese sausage 1

Garlic 3 cloves, peeled and finely chopped

Coriander (cilantro) root 1

Cooking oil 1 Tbsp

Butter 1 Tbsp

Red curry paste (see page 113) ¹/₂ tsp

Boneless chicken breast
  100 g (3¹/₂ oz), diced

Shallot 1, peeled and finely sliced

Curry powder 1 Tbsp

Steamed white rice 280 g (10 oz), chilled

Pork floss 2 Tbsp

Coriander (cilantro) leaves a handful

Red chilli 1, finely sliced

Toasted pine nuts 30 g (1 oz)

Seasoning

Salt ¹/₂ tsp

Sugar a pinch

Ground white pepper a pinch

1 To dice a whole pineapple, cut the top and bottom of, then halve it vertically. Slice off the skin, then cut flesh into cubes.

2 Parboil Chinese sausage in hot water for a few minutes before cutting into small cubes.

3 Using a mortar and pestle, pound garlic and coriander root into a fine paste.

4 Heat oil in a pan over medium heat. Add butter, red curry paste and garlic and coriander paste. Stir-fry until fragrant.

5 Add chicken and Chinese sausage. Stir-fry for a few minutes, then add the pineapple cubes, shallots and curry powder. Mix well.

6 Add the steamed rice and seasoning. Using the spatula to break up any lumps of rice, cook until rice is heated through.

7 Serve garnished with pork floss, coriander leaves, sliced red chilli and toasted pine nuts.

claypot prawn vermicelli goong ob woon-sen

A Thai claypot dish that has a unique combination of sauces and spices. Serves 4

Garlic 5 cloves, peeled

Coriander (cilantro) roots 2

White peppercorns 10

Red chilli 1, finely cut into strips

Cooking oil 2 Tbsp

Glass noodles 500 g (1 lb 1½ oz), soaked to soften and drained

Pork belly 50 g (1¾ oz), cut into 6 thin slices

Prawns (shrimps) 200 g (7 oz)

Spring onions (scallion) 2, cut into 1-cm (½-in) lengths

Seasoning

Maggi seasoning sauce 1 Tbsp

Oyster sauce 1 Tbsp

Chinese cooking wine 1 Tbsp

Chicken or vegetable stock (see page 112) 85 ml (2 ½ fl oz / ⅓ cup)

1 Using a mortar and pestle, pound 3 cloves garlic, coriander roots and white peppercorns into a fine paste. Combine paste with seasoning and chilli strips in a mixing bowl. Mix well and set aside.

2 Coat the inner walls of the claypot with cooking oil. Layer the ingredients in the pot. Cover the base with 3 slices of pork, then top with half the noodles and half the prawns. Repeat with the remaining ingredients.

3 Place remaining garlic cloves and spring onion on top, then pour seasoning over. Cover claypot with a lid and place over medium heat for 7–10 minutes, or until ingredients are cooked.

4 Serve hot, garnished as desired.

prawn paste rice kao krok ka-pi

Tasty and filling, this is a common lunch favourite among busy executives in Bangkok. **Serves 4**

Steamed rice 700 g (1½ lb)

Prawn (shrimp) paste 1 Tbsp

Lime 1, cut into quarters

Pork belly

Pork belly 500 g (1 lb 1½ oz)

Garlic 5 cloves, peeled

Coriander (cilantro) root 1

Ground white pepper ½ tsp

Palm sugar 3 Tbsp

Fish sauce 2 Tbsp

Dark soy sauce 1 Tbsp

Side dishes

Water 250 ml (8 fl oz / 1 cup)

Green mango 150 g (5⅓ oz), peeled and cut into strips

Shallots 3, peeled and finely sliced

Ground dried prawns (shrimps) 70 g (2½ oz)

Bird's eye chillies 2, finely chopped

Cashew nuts 140 g (5 oz), lightly toasted

Coriander (cilantro) leaves a handful

Eggs 2, cooked into an omelette and sliced

1   Slice the pork belly into 2.5-cm (1-in) thick slices.

2   Using a mortar and pestle, pound garlic, coriander root and pepper into a fine paste. Heat a pan over medium heat and dry-fry paste until fragrant.

3   Add pork belly, sugar, fish sauce and dark soy sauce and continue to stir-fry until pork belly is cooked.

4   Add water and stir well. Reduce to low heat and simmer until gravy has reduced and pork belly is tender. Remove from heat and set aside.

5   Using a clean pan, dry-fry prawn paste until fragrant. Remove from heat and mix well with steamed rice to get an even flavour and colour.

6   Serve rice by scooping it onto a plate, drizzling a spoonful or two of gravy over it, and arranging the pork belly pieces, side dishes and a few wedges of lime on the side.

meat and poultry

galangal chicken soup 53

minced pork bread triangles 54

stuffed omelette 57

clear soup with stuffed chinese cabbage 58

fried hard-boiled eggs with sweet shallot sauce 61

minced pork with fresh herbs 62

dry beef and lychee curry 65

roasted lemon grass chicken 66

deep-fried sun-dried pork strips 69

red curry roasted duck 70

golden corn cups 73

galangal chicken soup tom kha gai

A coconut-based soup flavoured with the refreshing tastes of galangal, lemon grass and kaffir lime leaves. Serves 4

Hon shimeji mushrooms 200 g (7 oz)

Coconut milk 750 ml (24 fl oz / 3 cups)

Lemon grass 1 stalk, bruised and cut into short lengths

Kaffir lime leaves 4

Galangal (preferably young roots) 2.5-cm (1-in) knob, peeled and sliced

Chicken thighs 6, sliced or 400 g (14$^1/_3$ oz) chicken breast, diced

Coconut cream 60 ml (2 fl oz / $^1/_4$ cup)

Lime juice 3 Tbsp

Fish sauce 2 Tbsp

Red bird's eye chillies 3, bruised

Red chilli 1, finely sliced

1 Separate hon shimeji mushrooms. Brush them lightly to remove any dirt. Set aside.

2 Bring coconut milk to the boil over medium heat. Add lemon grass, kaffir lime leaves and galangal slices.

3 Return coconut milk to the boil, then add chicken and cook until chicken changes colour and is cooked before adding mushrooms.

4 Stir in coconut cream. Add lime juice, fish sauce and chillies. Stir well.

5 Serve hot.

minced pork bread triangles
kha nom-pang na moo

This tasty, golden-brown snack is a tea-time favourite for both young and old in Thailand. Serves 4

Dry white bread 3 slices

Coriander (cilantro) root 1 sprig

Garlic 5 cloves, peeled and finely chopped

Ground white pepper ¹/₂ tsp

Minced pork 300 g (10¹/₂ oz)

Fish sauce 2 tsp

Sugar 1 tsp

Eggs 2, beaten

Vegetable oil for deep-frying

Coriander (cilantro) leaves a handful

Dipping Sauce

White vinegar 60 ml (2 fl oz / ¹/₄ cup)

Sugar 70 g (2¹/₂ oz)

Salt to taste

Water 125 ml (4 fl oz / ¹/₂ cup)

Cucumber 1, finely sliced

Red chilli 1, finely sliced into strips

Shallots 2, peeled and finely sliced

Carrot 1, diced

1 Cut each slice of bread into 4 small squares, then cut each square into 2 triangles.

2 Prepare dipping sauce. Combine vinegar, sugar, salt and water and stir until sugar dissolves.

3 Place cucumber, chilli, shallots and carrot into a pan and pour vinegar mixture over. Boil over medium heat for 5 minutes, then set aside to cool.

4 Using a mortar and pestle, pound coriander root and garlic into a fine paste. Add pepper and mix well. Transfer to a large bowl and mix well with minced pork, fish sauce, sugar and coriander leaves.

5 Spread 1 tsp of minced pork mixture over each bread triangle.

6 Heat oil for deep-frying over medium heat. Dip bread triangles topping side down in beaten egg, then deep-fry until golden brown. Remove and drain well. Serve with dipping sauce.

stuffed omelette kad yud sai

A savoury, fragrant dish with a minced meat filling that is quick and easy to prepare. **Serves 2**

Eggs 3

Cooking oil 2 Tbsp

Garlic 3 cloves, peeled and finely chopped

Minced meat (chicken, pork or beef) 200 g (7 oz)

Carrot 1, diced

Tomatoes 2, diced

Shallots 2, peeled and finely chopped

Corn flour (cornstarch) 1 Tbsp, mixed with 2 Tsbp water

Spring onion (scallion) 1, finely chopped

Seasoning

Sugar 1 tsp

Salt 1 tsp

Ground white pepper 1 tsp

1 Beat eggs well, then divide into 2 portions. Heat ¹/₂ Tbsp oil in a non-stick pan over medium heat. Pour a portion of egg into pan and swirl pan so egg coats base of pan. Allow egg to cook completely., then repeat with remaining egg. Remove from heat and lay each omelette in a small rice bowl with edge hanging out. Set aside.

2 Heat remaining cooking oil over medium heat. Add garlic and stir-fry until fragrant.

3 Add minced meat and carrot. Stir-fry for a few minutes, then add tomatoes, shallots and seasoning. Continue to stir-fry until minced meat is cooked and carrot is tender.

4 Add cornflour mixture to thicken gravy. Stir-fry for a few minutes, then remove from heat and add chopped spring onions.

5 Spoon half the minced meat into each omelette and make a parcel by flipping edges of egg over minced meat.

6 Place an overturned plate over each omelette parcel, then turn bowl over so omelette falls onto plate. Garnish as desired and serve with 2 bowls of steamed rice.

clear soup with stuffed chinese cabbage
gaeng jued pak kard yad sai

A clear, peppery broth that can be served as an appetiser or as a light main course. **Serves 4**

Chinese cabbage 6 leaves, large

Chicken or vegetable stock (see page 112) 1 litre (32 fl oz / 4 cups)

Fish sauce 2 Tbsp

Sugar a pinch

Ground white pepper ¹/₂ tsp

Preserved salted radish 1 tsp

Spring onions (scallion) 2, cut into 2.5-cm (1-inch) lengths

Crisp-fried shallots 2 tsp

Filling

Coriander (cilantro) roots 2, chopped

Garlic 3 cloves, peeled and finely chopped

Cornflour (cornstarch) ¹/₂ tsp

Salt ¹/₂ tsp

Sugar 1 tsp

Minced pork 400 g (14¹/₃ oz)

Ground white pepper a pinch

1   Bring a pot of lightly salted water to the boil. Blanch cabbage leaves for 3 minutes, then drain and plunge into a basin of ice water.

2   Drain cabbage leaves, cut stems off and leave aside.

3   Prepare filling. Combine coriander root, garlic, corn flour, salt, white pepper and sugar in a bowl. Add minced pork and mix well. Divide into 6 portions.

4   Spoon a portion of minced pork onto the centre of each cabbage leaf. Bring opposite sides of leaf up over filling, then roll up like a spring roll. Repeat this step to make 5 more cabbage parcels.

5   Place cabbage parcels on a steaming plate and steam for 5 minutes over high heat.

6   Bring stock to boil, then add carefully lower in cabbage parcels.

7   Add fish sauce, sugar, white pepper and preserved cabbage. Serve garnished with spring onions and fried shallots.

fried hard-boiled eggs with
sweet shallot sauce kai look khey

Otherwise known as "Son-in-law's eggs", this is an incredibly simple dish that doubles up as a snack or main dish. Serves 4

Hard-boiled eggs 4

Cooking oil for deep frying

Sauce

Shallots 2, peeled and finely sliced

Water 2 Tbsp

Tamarind juice (see page 113) 2 Tbsp

Fish sauce 1 Tbsp

Palm sugar 1 Tbsp

1   Carefully peel shells off hard-boiled eggs, being careful not to break eggs.

2   Heat oil for deep-frying. Carefully lower eggs into hot oil and fry golden brown in colour. Drain well and set aside.

3   Heat 2 Tbsp oil in a pan and cook shallots until lightly browned. Remove and set aside to drain and cool. Prepare more and store in an airtight jar. Use to garnish meat or rice dishes.

4   Add water, tamarind juice, fish sauce and palm sugar to a separate pot over low heat. Add deep-fried shallots and simmer for 3–4 minutes or until shallot sauce thickens slightly.

5   Serve deep-fried eggs drizzled with shallot sauce.

minced pork with fresh herbs larb moo

A fragrant dish that combines the fresh flavours of basil and mint leaves, crunchy vegetables and toasted ground rice. Serves 4

Glutinous rice 140 g (5 oz)

Kaffir lime leaves a handful

Galangal 2.5-cm (1-in) knob, peeled and finely sliced

Chicken stock or water (see page 112) 250 ml (8 fl oz / 1 cup)

Minced pork 200 g (7 oz)

Shallots 2, peeled and finely sliced

Dried chilli powder 1 Tbsp

Chopped spring onion (scallion) 1 Tbsp

Sawtooth coriander 1 sprig, finely chopped

Mint leaves a handful, freshly picked

Basil leaves a handful, freshly picked

Cucumber 1, finely sliced

Butterhead lettuce 1 head

Seasoning

Lime juice 2 Tbsp

Fish sauce 1 Tbsp

Sugar 1 tsp

1   Heat a saucepan over medium heat. Add glutinous rice, kaffir lime leaves and galangal slices. Dry-fry until rice grains turn golden brown in colour. Remove kaffir lime leaves and galangal slices.

2   Using a mortar and pestle, pound toasted rice grains into a fine paste. Set 1 Tbsp ground rice aside and store remaining rice in an airtight container for future use.

3   Bring chicken stock or water to the boil over medium heat. Add minced pork, shallots, 1 Tbsp ground rice and dried chilli powder. Add seasoning. Stir-fry quickly until minced pork is cooked.

4   Remove minced pork mixture from heat and mix with spring onion and sawtooth coriander.

5   Serve immediately with mint leaves, basil leaves, cucumber and butterhead lettuce on the side.

This dish must be served immediately so the flavour of the fresh herbs can be enjoyed.

dry beef and lychee curry pa nang nuea

A Thai intepretation of the Malay dry beef curry *(rendang)*, this dish is additionally sweetened with large and juicy Thai lychees. Serves 4

Beef loin 300 g (10¹/₂ oz)

Cooking oil 2 Tbsp

Red curry paste (see page 113) 1 Tbsp

Coconut cream 250 ml (8 fl oz / 1 cup)

Thai lychees 10, peeled and seeded, or use canned lychees

Red chillies 2, finely sliced

Kaffir lime leaves 4, finely sliced

Basil leaves a handful

Seasoning

Fish sauce 1 Tbsp

Sugar ¹/₂ Tbsp

1   Cut beef loin into medium-fine slices.

2   Heat cooking oil over medium heat. Add red curry paste and stir-fry until fragrant.

3   Add beef slices and stir-fry to coat beef with paste. Stir in coconut cream, mixing well.

4   Lower heat and simmer until curry is reduced and thick. Add seasoning and stir. Add lychees and remove from heat.

5   Serve immediately, garnished with red chilli, kaffir lime leaves and basil leaves.

If a tougher cut of beef is used, tenderise with a little oil and corn flour for half an hour before cooking.

roasted lemon grass chicken gai ob ta khai

A succulent dish of roasted chicken with a savoury, lemony twist. Serves 4

Chicken thighs 4

Lemon grass 3 stalks

Cooking oil 2 Tbsp

Marinade

Lemon grass 4 stalks, ends trimmed
and bruised

Dark soy sauce 1 Tbsp

Light soy sauce 1 Tbsp

Oyster sauce 2 Tbsp

Fish sauce 1 Tbsp

Water 125 ml (4 fl oz / ½ cup)

Garnish (optional)

Cooking oil for deep-frying

Lemon grass 2 stalks, ends trimmed,
finely sliced

1   Prepare this dish a day ahead or least 3–4 hours before serving.

2   Chop lemon grass finely. Heat a saucepan over medium heat. Add lemon grass and ingredients for marinade and bring to the boil. Remove from heat, cover saucepan with a lid and leave until completely cool.

3   When marinade is cool, transfer to a mixing bowl. Place chicken in to steep in the marinade. Leave for 3–4 hours or overnight in the refrigerator.

4   Preheat oven to 220°C (440°F).

5   Arrange chicken thighs on a baking tray. Dip bruised lemon grass stalks in oil and brush chicken thighs. Place chicken thighs in preheated oven for 12–15 minutes.

6   Meanwhile, prepare garnish if desired. Heat oil for deep-frying, then deep-fry finely sliced lemon grass until crisp and golden brown. Set aside to drain well.

7   Remove chicken thighs from oven and place on a serving plate. Drain drippings from baking tray and serve as a dipping sauce. Serve immediately, garnished with deep-fried lemon grass, if using.

deep-fried sun-dried pork moo dad diaw

Often consumed in the evening as a prelude to dinner in Thailand, this tasty dish is the perfect accompaniment to a light, refreshing Thai beer. **Serves 4**

Pork shoulder 1 kg (2 lb 3 oz), cut into 1 x 5-cm ($^1/_2$ x 2-in) strips

Cooking oil for deep-frying

Cucumber or carrot 1, cut into 0.5 x 4-cm ($^1/_4$ x 1$^1/_2$-in) strips

Marinade

Fish sauce 90 ml (3 fl oz / $^3/_8$ cup)

Sugar 150 g (5$^1/_3$ oz)

Ground coriander 1 Tbsp

1   Prepare marinade. Mix fish sauce, sugar and ground coriander seed powder well in a mixing bowl.

2   Place pork strips in marinade and leave to steep for 1 hour.

3   Arrange pork strips on a baking tray or rack and leave to air-dry in a sunny, breezy place for 2 hours.

4   Heat oil for deep-frying over medium heat and deep-fry pork strips until golden brown. Drain and set aside. Serve with cucumber or carrot strips.

red curry roasted duck gaeng phed ped yaang

This dish was prepared only for Thai royalty in the past, but it has now become a popular family throughout central Thailand. **Serves 4**

Roast duck breast 1, medium-sized

Aubergine (eggplant) 1

Coconut cream 250 ml (8 fl oz / 1 cup)

Red curry paste (see page 113) 2 Tbsp

Kaffir lime leaves 5, finely sliced (reserve some for garnish)

Lemon grass 1 stalk

Coconut milk 500 ml (16 fl oz / 2 cups)

Cherry tomatoes 5, halved

Red chillies 2, finely sliced into strips

Thai basil leaves 110 g (4 oz)

Seasoning

Fish sauce 2 Tbsp

Palm sugar or white sugar 1/2 Tbsp

1 Cut duck breast into thin slices and set aside.

2 Finely dice aubergine, then soak in salt water to prevent oxidisation. Set aside.

3 Bring coconut cream to the boil, stirring well to prevent burning.

4 Add red curry paste, kaffir lime leaves and lemon grass. Cook, stirring until fragrant. Remove kaffir lime leaves and lemon grass.

5 Add coconut milk and return mixture to the boil.

6 Add drained aubergine pieces and cherry tomatoes. Cook until aubergine is tender.

7 Add roast duck slices, seasoning and red chillies. Stir well and remove from heat. Garnish with basil leaves, reserved kaffir lime leaves and serve with a bowl of steamed rice.

golden corn cups kra-tong thong

Tender, juicy chicken and corn kernels in crispy, golden cups make a great tea-time snack. **Serves about 10**

Pastry cup

Plain (all-purpose) flour 140 g (5 oz)

Rice flour 30 g (1 oz)

Eggs 2

Water 375 ml (12 fl oz / 1¹/₂ cups)

Cooking oil for deep-frying

Pastry mould (tin or brass)

Coriander (cilantro) leaves a handful

Filling

Garlic 3 cloves, peeled

Coriander (cilantro) root 1

Curry powder ¹/₂ Tbsp

Ground white pepper ¹/₂ tsp

Cooking oil 1 Tbsp

Boneless chicken breast 200 g (7 oz), finely diced

Corn kernels 280 g (10 oz)

Shallots 2, peeled and finely sliced

Sugar 2 Tbsp

Salt ¹/₂ tsp

1 Combine plain flour, rice flour, eggs and water in a mixing bowl and whisk into a fine batter.

2 Heat cooking oil for deep-frying. Submerge cups of pastry mould into hot oil for a few seconds. Remove, dip cups quickly into batter and place them in hot oil.

3 Deep-fry until pastry cups become golden brown in colour. Drain well and set aside. Store excess cups in an airtight container for future use.

4 Prepare the filling. Using a mortar and pestle, combine garlic, coriander root, curry powder and pepper and pound into a fine paste.

5 Heat cooking oil over medium heat. Add paste, chicken, corn kernels and shallots. Stir-fry until chicken is cooked. Add sugar and salt and remove from heat.

6 Spoon filling into pastry cups and serve immediately, garnished with coriander leaves.

fish and seafood

rice crackers with prawn and pork peanut sauce 76

steamed fish with lime and lemon grass sauce 79

stuffed squid in green curry 80

sour prawns and papaya curry 83

steamed fish mousse with blue mussels 84

tom yum prawns 87

deep-fried fish with tamarind sauce 88

'fluffy' fish with mango sauce 91

rice crackers with prawn and
pork peanut sauce khao tung na tang

Brighten up a party or casual meal with this savoury, nutty dip made with prawns and minced pork. **Serves 4**

Cooking oil for deep-frying

Rice crackers 20

Prawns (shrimps) 300 g (11 oz), peeled

Minced pork 300 g (10½ oz)

Dipping sauce

Coriander (cilantro) roots 2, finely chopped

Dried chillies 2, soaked and seeded

Garlic 5 cloves, peeled and finely chopped

Ground white pepper 1 tsp

Coconut cream 500 ml (16 fl oz / 2 cups)

Peanuts 70 g (2½ oz), toasted and ground

Shallots 2, peeled and finely chopped

Water 250 ml (8 fl oz / 1 cup)

Fish sauce 2 Tbsp

Sugar 2 Tbsp

Tamarind juice (see page 113) 2 Tbsp

1 Heat oil for deep-frying over medium heat. Deep-fry rice crackers until light golden brown in colour. Drain well and set aside.

2 Mince prawns using a chef's knife or cleaver.

3 Use a mortar and pestle to pound coriander roots, dried chillies, garlic and pepper into a fine paste.

4 Bring half the coconut cream to the boil over medium heat. Add coriander paste and stir well, then add minced prawns and pork.

5 Add remaining coconut cream, peanuts shallots and water. Bring to the boil, stirring. Add fish sauce, sugar and tamarind juice. Reduce to low heat and allow dipping sauce to simmer until thick.

6 Serve rice crackers with dipping sauce, garnished as desired.

Stir the sauce continuously to prevent it from burning. Any remaining sauce can be kept in the freezer and warmed up on the stove or in the microwave oven.

steamed fish with lime and
lemon grass sauce pla neng ma now

The sweetness of the fish is heightened with the use of simple but fragrant
Thai ingredients such as lemon grass and galangal. Serves up to 5

Sea bass 500 g (1 lb 1½ oz), cleaned
and gutted

Lemon grass 5 stalks

Lime 1, thinly sliced

Lime and lemon grass sauce

Lemon grass 1 stalk

Bird's eye chillies 2, sliced

Chicken stock (see page 112) 250 ml
(8 fl oz / 1 cup)

Finely chopped Chinese celery 2 Tbsp

Fish sauce 1 Tbsp

Galangal 2.5-cm (1-in) knob, peeled
and sliced

Garlic 5 cloves, peeled and finely chopped

Ground white pepper 1 tsp

Lime juice 2 Tbsp

Sugar to taste

1 Cut lemon grass into short lengths and bruise them slightly. Arrange
   them like a bed on a shallow plate for steaming sea bass. Place sea bass
   on top of the lemon grass bed.

2 Prepare lime and lemon grass sauce by chopping lemon grass finely.
   Combine with remaining sauce ingredients in a mixing bowl and mix well.

3 Place lime slices on sea bass and pour sauce over. Steam sea bass over
   high heat for 8–10 minutes. Serve immediately.

stuffed squid in green curry
gaeng khiew wan pla muek yud sai

A southern Thai seafood curry that is pleasantly flavoured and spiced with basil, chillies and peppercorns. **Serves 4**

Squid 500 g (1 lb 1¹/₂ oz)

Green curry paste (see page 113) 2 Tbsp

Coconut cream 250 ml (8 fl oz / 1 cup)

Coconut milk 500 ml (16 fl oz / 2 cups)

Aubergine (eggplant) 70 g (2¹/₂ oz), diced

Basil leaves a handful

Red chillies 2, finely sliced into strips

Green peppercorns a handful

Filling

Minced pork 300 g (11 oz)

Green curry paste (see page 113) ¹/₂ tsp

Fish sauce 1 tsp

Sugar a pinch

Corn flour (cornstarch) ¹/₂ Tbsp

Coconut cream ¹/₂ Tbsp

Seasoning

Fish sauce 1–2 Tbsp

Palm sugar ¹/₂ Tbsp

1 Separate squid heads from bodies, rinse and set aside. Clean squid tubes by removing innards and pulling away as much of the skin as possible. Rinse well.

2 Combine filling ingredients and mix well. Spoon filling into squid tubes, then stuff heads in and secure with toothpicks.

3 Steam stuffed squids over high heat for about 7 minutes. Meanwhile, bring the coconut cream to the boil, then add the coconut milk and green curry paste. Stir until fragrant, then add aubergine pieces. Reduce to low heat and allow aubergine to cook until tender.

4 Add steamed squid, basil leaves, red chilli strips, peppercorns and seasoning. Cook for 1–2 minutes longer.

5 To serve, remove toothpicks from squid and serve immediately.

sour prawns and papaya curry
gaeng som ma ra kor

A spicy, sour curry flavoured with notes of tamarind and papaya. **Serves 4**

Green papaya 1

Vegetable stock (see page 112) 750 ml
(24 fl oz / 3 cups)

Prawns (shrimps) 300 g (11 oz), peeled

Coriander (cilantro) leaves a handful

Red chilli 1, finely sliced into strips

Paste

Dried chillies 5–7, seeded and soaked

Dried prawns (shrimps) 1 Tbsp, ground

Fish sauce 2 Tbsp

Chinese keys 2.5-cm (1-in) knob, peeled
and finely chopped

Finely chopped shallots 1 Tbsp

Prawn (shrimp) paste 1 tsp

Sugar a pinch

Tamarind juice (see page 113) 60 ml
(2 fl oz / ¼ cup)

1 Using a sharp knife, slice skin off papaya. Cut papaya across in half, then dig out any seeds. Cut papaya into medium-fine strips.

2 Bring stock to the boil over medium heat. Meanwhile, use a blender (food processor) to blend paste ingredients into a fine paste. Add stock and return to the boil.

3 Add papaya and prawns to stock. Return to the boil again, then reduce to low heat and allow to simmer until papaya turns translucent.

4 Serve garnished with coriander leaves and red chilli strips.

steamed fish mousse with blue mussels
hor mok hoi mang poo

A creamy, delicately flavoured fish paste steamed in blue mussel shells. **Serves 4**

Mackerel or yellow tail 300 g (11 oz)

Coconut cream 750 ml (24 fl oz / 3 cups)

Egg 1

Kaffir lime leaves 3, finely sliced

Red curry paste (see page 113) 1 Tbsp

Blue mussels 1 kg (2 lb 3 oz)

Red chillies 2, finely sliced into strips

Seasoning

Fish sauce 3 Tbsp

Palm sugar 1 tsp

Garnishing

Coconut cream 2 Tbsp

Kaffir lime leaf 1, finely sliced

Red chilli 1, finely sliced into strips

1 Fillet fish (see page 40). Scrape meat off fillets using a spoon, then mash lightly to break meat up further.

2 Add minced fish, coconut cream, egg, kaffir lime leaves, red curry paste and seasoning to a mixing bowl and mix well into a paste.

3 Bring a pot of water to the boil and poach mussels until they open. Drain and break top shells off mussels. Discard any that do not open.

4 Spread 1 Tbsp fish paste over mussels, creating a slight mound. Steam over high heat for approximately 5 minutes and drizzle a few drops of coconut cream over each mussel.

5 Serve garnished with red chilli strips and kaffir lime leaf strips.

tom yum prawns tom yum goong

This clear, spicy broth is flavoured with lemon grass, coriander and galangal. Serves 4

Lemon grass 2 stalks

Chicken stock (see page 112) 1.25 litres (40 fl oz / 5 cups)

Bird's eye chillies 2–3, bruised and sliced

Coriander (cilantro) root 1, bruised

Galangal 2.5-cm (1-in) knob, peeled and finely sliced

Kaffir lime leaves 4–5, torn into halves

Prawns (shrimps) 400 g (14$^1/_3$ oz), peeled

Straw or abalone mushrooms 100 g (3$^1/_2$ oz), finely sliced

Coriander (cilantro) leaves 1 sprig

Seasoning

Lime juice 5 Tbsp

Fish sauce 3 Tbsp

Thai tom yum paste (optional) 1 Tbsp

1   Bruise bulbous ends of lemon grass stalks using the handle of a knife. Cut lemon grass into short lengths.

2   Bring chicken stock to the boil over medium heat. Add bird's eye chillies, coriander root, galangal, kaffir lime leaves and lemon grass segments. Return stock to the boil for another 5 minutes.

3   Scoop out coriander root, galangal, kaffir lime leaves and lemon grass segments. Add prawns and mushrooms and return to the boil again, until prawns are cooked. Add seasoning and remove from heat.

4   Serve garnished with coriander leaves.

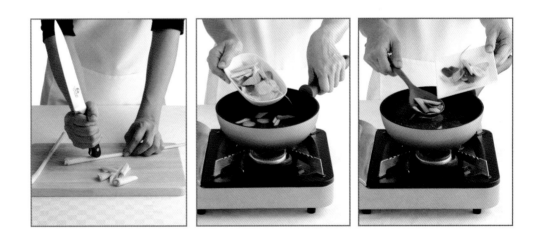

deep-fried fish with tamarind sauce
pla sam rod

Crispy, battered fish topped with a sweet, tangy sauce. **Serves 3–5**

Red snapper (or any white-fleshed fish)
  300 g (11 oz)

Coriander (cilantro) leaves 1 sprig

Garlic 10 cloves, peeled

Red chillies 3–5, finely sliced

Cooking oil for deep-frying

Plain (all-purpose) flour for coating

Roasted black sesame seeds a handful

Tamarind sauce

Tamarind juice (see page 113) 125 ml
  (4 fl oz / ½ cup)

Palm sugar 1 Tbsp

Fish sauce 1 Tbsp

Water 2 Tbsp

1 Fillet fish (see page 40). Cut fillets into 4-cm (1½-in) slices.

2 Use a mortar and pestle and pound coriander, garlic and red chillies into a fine paste. Heat a saucepan over medium heat and stir-fry paste until fragrant. Add ingredients for tamarind sauce and reduce to low heat. Continue to stir until paste thickens. Remove from heat and set aside.

3 Heat cooking oil for deep-frying. Coat fish slices with plain flour, then deep-fry until crisp and light golden brown in colour. Drain well and set aside.

4 Ladle tamarind sauce over fish slices. Serve garnished with roasted sesame seeds.

'fluffy' fish with mango sauce
yum pla dook foo

A northeastern dish of crispy catfish flavoured with a light, tangy sauce. **Serves 4**

Cured, roasted catfish (or any white-fleshed fish in similar form) 1.5 kg (3 lb 4¹/₂ oz), deboned

Cooking oil for deep-frying

Roasted cashew nuts a handful

Coriander (cilantro) leaves a handful

Mango sauce

Fish sauce 2 Tbsp

Green mango 1, peeled and finely sliced into strips (reserve some for garnish)

Lime juice 4 Tbsp

Red chillies 2, finely chopped and seeded

Shallots 4, peeled and finely diced

Sugar ¹/₂ tsp

1   Use your hands to break fish into small pieces.

2   Heat cooking oil for deep-frying and deep-fry fish until crisp and golden brown in colour. Drain well and set aside to cool. Once cooled, chop fish up finely to obtain a "fluffy" texture.

3   Combine mango sauce ingredients in a mixing bowl and mix well. Drizzle sauce over fish.

4   Serve fish garnished with reserved mango strips, roasted cashew nuts and coriander leaves.

desserts

glutinous rice with ripe mango 94

egg custard pumpkin 97

red rubies 98

tapioca cake 101

lemon grass jelly with lime sherbet 102

bananas simmered in coconut milk 105

water chestnut cake in screwpine leaf cups 106

coconut ice cream 109

glutinous rice with ripe mango
khao niew ma muang

The sweetness of ripened mangoes is heightened by lightly salted glutinous rice and coconut milk in this simple dessert. **Serves 4**

Glutinous rice 3 cups, washed and soaked overnight or for at least 4 hours

Muslin cloth 30 x 30-cm (12 x 12-in) square

Coconut cream 250 ml (8 fl oz / 1 cup)

Fresh coconut juice or water 125 ml (4 fl oz / ½ cup)

Screwpine (pandan) leaves 2–3, knotted

Sugar 140 g (5 oz)

Salt 1 Tbsp

Cooking oil 1 Tbsp

Ripe mangoes 3–4, cubed

Roasted black sesame seeds 1 tsp

1   Drain glutinous rice. Place muslin cloth over a steaming plate, then spoon rice onto plate. Steam over medium heat for 30 minutes.

2   Combine coconut cream and juice or water, screwpine leaves, sugar and salt to make the coconut sauce. Bring to the boil for 2–3 minutes, preferably during the last 5 minutes of steaming glutinous rice.

3   Place steamed glutinous rice into a pot. Mix well with oil, then pour coconut sauce over.

4   Quickly stir coconut sauce into steamed glutinous rice and cover pot with a lid. Place over medium heat and allow rice to simmer for about 30 minutes. Give the rice a quick stir again and remove from heat.

5   Shape glutinous rice into small mounds. Sprinkle with sesame seeds and serve with mango.

egg custard pumpkin sang kaya fuk thong

A simple dessert of creamy, sweet custard that can be enjoyed
freshly steamed or chilled. **Serves 4**

Pumpkin 1, 500 g (1 lb 1½ oz)

Eggs 4

Fresh milk 60 ml (2 fl oz / ¼ cup)

Coconut cream 125 ml (4 fl oz / ½ cup)

Palm sugar or white sugar 100 g (3½ oz)

Vanilla essence ½ tsp

Screwpine *(pandan)* leaves 2–3, knotted

1   Cut top off pumpkin, then scoop out seeds.

2   Break eggs into a mixing bowl and add fresh milk, coconut cream, sugar
    and vanilla essence. Use the screwpine leaves to blend the egg custard
    mixture.

3   Pour egg custard mixture into pumpkin and steam, covered, over medium
    heat for 1 hour.

4   Serve warm or refrigerate and serve chilled.

red rubies tup tip grob

An attractive dessert of crunchy water chestnuts encased in a clear, starchy coating, and served with sweetened coconut sauce. **Serves 4**

Water chestnuts 140 g (5 oz)

Red food colouring 1 tsp

Tapioca flour 280 g (10 oz)

Water 2 litres (64 fl oz / 3$^1/_5$ pints)

Coconut cream 250 ml (8 fl oz / 1 cup)

Sugar 100 g (3$^1/_2$ oz)

Chopped jackfruit or any other fruit (optional) 100 g (3$^1/_2$ oz)

1 Peel skin off water chesnuts, then cut into small cubes. Stir red food colouring into 250 ml (8 fl oz / 1 cup) water and place water chestnuts in to soak for 1 hour.

2 Drain water chestnuts, then coat well with tapioca flour.

3 Bring water to the boil. Add coated water chestnuts and continue to boil until water chestnuts float to the surface. Remove with a sieve and plunge immediately into ice water.

4 To make coconut sauce, combine coconut cream and sugar, and bring to the boil for 2–3 minutes. Set aside to cool.

5 Drizzle coconut sauce over water chestnuts and serve topped with fruit, if desired.

tapioca cake kha-nom-man

Grating the tapioca may take some effort, but these soft, candied tapioca cakes are worth it! **Serves 4**

Tapioca (cassava) root 1, medium

Water 250 ml (8 fl oz / 1 cup)

Sugar 140 g (5 oz)

Red food colouring 1–2 tsp

Jasmine essence 1–2 drops

Grated skinned coconut 140 g (5 oz)

1 Peel tapioca, then grate into a mixing bowl.

2 Add remaining ingredients, except grated coconut, to grated tapioca and mix well. Pour mixture into a deep tray for steaming.

3 Steam over medium heat for 25–30 minutes until mixture is set. Remove from heat and set aside to cool, then cut tapioca cake into any shape of your preference.

4 Coat tapioca cake with grated coconut and serve immediately.

lemongrass jelly with lime sherbet
woon ta khai

A lemony gelatinous dessert with the refreshing zing of lime sherbet and zest. Perfect after a spicy meal or on a hot day. **Serves 4**

Lemon grass 10 stalks, bruised and chopped

Kaffir lime leaves 4–5

Screwpine (pandan) leaves 3, knotted

Mint leaves a handful

Water 3 litres (96 fl oz / 12 cups)

Gelatine powder 40 g (1³/₄ oz)

Sugar 500 g (1 lb 1¹/₂ oz)

Lime sherbet (or any other flavour) 4 scoops

Lime zest 1 tsp

1 Combine lemon grass, kaffir lime leaves, screwpine leaves, mint leaves and water in a large pot and bring to the boil over medium heat. Once mixture comes to the boil, reduce to low heat and allow to simmer for 1 hour, covered. Remove from heat and strain mixture back into the same pot.

2 Stir gelatine powder and sugar into pot and stir well until sugar dissolves.

3 Pour mixture into a mould and set aside to cool. Once cooled, refrigerate until jelly mixture is chilled and solidified.

4 Scoop lemon grass jelly into small cups and top with lime sherbet. Serve garnished with mint leaves and lime zest.

bananas simmered in coconut milk
gluaw buad chee

The sweetness of bananas blend perfectly with warm coconut milk.
A simple and quick dessert to end any meal. **Serves 4**

Half-ripe small bananas 4–5

Coconut milk 750 ml (24 fl oz / 3 cups)

Sugar 70 g (2¹/₂ oz)

Salt ¹/₄ tsp

Screwpine (*pandan*) leaves 2, knotted

Coconut cream (optional) 2 Tbsp

1 Peel bananas. Cut ends off for better presentation, if desired. Set aside.

2 Combine coconut milk, sugar and salt in a pot and bring to the boil over medium heat, stirring until sugar dissolves completely.

3 Add bananas and screwpine leaves and return to the boil. Reduce to low heat and allow to simmer for 10 minutes.

4 Slice bananas and serve warm in coconut milk sauce. Drizzle with coconut cream, if desired.

water chestnut cake in
screwpine leaf cups ta koo

These screwpine leaf cups are not only pretty, they also impart a light fragrance to this sweet, creamy dessert of crunchy water chestnuts layered with coconut mousse. **Serves up to 10**

Bottom layer

Screwpine (*pandan*) leaves 10, cut into short lengths

Water 1 litre (32 fl oz / 4 cups)

Muslin cloth 30 x 30-cm (12 x 12-in) square

Green bean flour 2 Tbsp

Rice flour 70 g (2$^{1}/_{2}$ oz)

Tapioca flour 30 g (1 oz)

Sugar 100 g (3$^{1}/_{2}$ oz)

Water chestnuts 140 g (5 oz), peeled and finely chopped

Screwpine leaf cups

Screwpine (*pandan*) leaves 10–15

Top layer

Coconut cream 500 ml (16 fl oz / 2 cups)

Rice flour 1 Tbsp

Green bean flour 1 Tbsp

Salt $^{1}/_{2}$ tsp

Sugar $^{1}/_{2}$ tsp

1 To make cups, cut leaves into 20-cm (8-in) lengths. Fold leaf at every 4-cm (1.5-in) interval.

2 Use a pair of scissors to make 4 small incisions up to the central vein of the leaf, and only on one side of the leaf. Use the folded lines as a guide. Trim edge of leaf, on cut side, a little.

3 Fold leaf into a square container as shown on the left. Secure leaf cups with fine bamboo slivers or thin toothpicks. Set aside.

4 Prepare bottom layer. Using a mortar and pestle, pound screwpine leaves, then add water and squeeze with your hands to extract the juice. Strain through a piece of muslin cloth into a pot. You should get 1 litre (32 fl oz / 4 cups) juice.

5 Add green bean flour, rice flour, tapioca flour and sugar to pot and mix well. Bring to the boil over medium to low heat, stirring well. Add water chestnuts and stir until liquid becomes translucent. Remove from heat and set aside to cool. Spoon cooled mixture into screwpine leaf cups, filling cups only halfway. Refrigerate until set.

6 To make the layer, combine ingredients and bring to the boil for 2–3 minutes until thickened. Spoon into screwpine leaf cups.

7 Refrigerate to chill before serving.

coconut ice cream ice cream krati

Richly flavoured with coconut cream and filled with tasty corn kernels, this decadent dessert will be a hit with both young and old. Serves 4

Coconut cream 500 ml (16 fl oz / 2 cups)

Sugar 140 g (5 oz)

Egg 1

Whipping cream 250 ml (8 fl oz / 1 cup)

Corn kernels 2 Tbsp

Diced jackfruit 2 Tbsp

Chopped peanuts 2 Tbsp

1   Bring coconut cream to the boil over medium heat, then add sugar and stir until sugar dissolves completely. Set aside to cool.

2   Crack egg into a mixing bowl, then whisk in whipping cream to get a firm mousse. Add the mousse to the coconut cream and mix well. Pour ice cream mixture into a freezing container, and freeze for 3–4 hours.

3   Remove ice cream from the freezer and spoon into a blender (food processor). Blend until smooth. If mixture is too frozen, add 1–2 Tbsp coconut cream to make the blending easier.

4   Add corn kernels and diced jackfruit to ice cream mixture and mix well. Return ice cream to the freezer for another 1–2 hours.

5   Serve ice cream on a bed of corn kernels or diced fresh fruit and garnish with chopped peanuts, if desired.

basic recipes

chicken stock

Makes 1 litre (32 fl oz / 4 cups)

Chicken bones or lean chicken meat 1 kg (2 lb 3 oz)

White onions 2, peeled and cut in half

Coriander (cilantro) roots 2

Salt 1 tsp

White peppercorns 5

Water 1 litre (32 fl oz / 4 cups)

1 Combine all ingredients in a large pot and bring to the boil over medium heat. Lower heat and simmer until stock turns clear. Return stock to the boil, then lower heat and simmer for another 1–1½ hours. Remove from heat and strain stock.

2 If not using immediately, leave stock to cool, then refrigerate for up to 4 days or freeze for up to 1 month. Defrost over low heat or in the microwave oven when needed.

vegetable stock

Makes 1 litre (32 fl oz / 4 cups)

Cabbage 1, small, leaves separated and roughly chopped

Carrots 2, peeled and cut into chunks

White onion 1, peeled and cut in half

Salt 1 tsp

Ground white pepper 1 tsp

Water 1 litre (32 fl oz / 4 cups)

1 Combine all ingredients in a large pot and bring to the boil over medium heat. Lower heat and simmer for 1 hour. Remove from heat and strain stock.

2 If not using immediately, leave stock to cool, then refrigerate for up to 4 days or freeze for up to 1 month. Defrost over low heat or in the microwave oven when needed.

red curry paste

makes about 2 cups

Ground coriander 1 Tbsp, dry-roasted

Ground cumin 1 tsp, dry-roasted

Lemon grass 2 stalks, finely sliced

Dried chillies 13, seeded and soaked

Galangal 2.5 cm (1-in) knob, peeled and finely chopped

Shallots 5, peeled and finely chopped

Garlic 15 cloves, peeled

Black peppercorns 20

Kaffir lime zest 1 tsp

Coriander (cilantro) roots 4, finely chopped

Prawn (shrimp) paste 1 tsp

green curry paste

makes about 2 cups

Ground coriander 1 Tbsp, dry-roasted

Ground cumin 1 tsp, dry-roasted

Lemon grass 2 stalks, finely sliced

Green bird's eye chillies 20

Galangal 10-cm (4-in) knob, peeled and finely sliced

Shallots 10, peeled and finely chopped

Garlic 15 cloves, peeled

Black peppercorns 10

Kaffir lime zest 1 tsp

Coriander (cilantro) roots 3, finely chopped

Prawn (shrimp) paste 1 tsp

Salt 1 tsp

1 Using a dry wok, fry ground coriander and cumin until fragrant. Set aside to cool.

2 Place lemon grass, chillies, galangal, shallots, garlic and peppercorns into a blender (food processor), and blend into a paste. Add remaining ingredients, ground coriander and cumin and blend to mix well.

These curry pastes can keep for up to 3 weeks in clean, dry, air tight containers in the refrigerator, or up to 2 months in the freezer.

tamarind juice

Makes about 300 ml (10 fl oz / 1¼ cups)

Tamarind pulp 1 Tbsp

Warm water 250 ml (4 fl oz / 1 cup)

1 Combine tamarind pulp and water in a small bowl. Use your fingers to knead and dissolve pulp. Strain juice and discard residue. Tamarind juice can keep for weeks refrigerated.

glossary

1. Fish sauce

Salty and strong in flavour, fish sauce is widely used in Thailand, to flavour dishes and also as a dipping sauce. Ranging from a light to dark reddish brown colour, fish sauce is made from a combination of fermented anchovies, salt and water. Fish sauce is available in Asian supermarkets.

2. Grated skinned coconut

Made by grating fresh skinned coconut flesh, grated skinned coconut is commonly used as a coating over Thai desserts. Grated coconut is also used to extract coconut cream or milk, after which the residue is tasteless and usually dicarded.

3. Palm sugar

Made from the sap of the coconut palm, palm sugar is sold either as solid blocks or slabs. Thai palm sugar tends to be light brown, with beige hues, whereas Indonesian or Malaysian varieties tend to be much darker in colour. Store away from heat and direct sunlight in an airtight container for a longer shelf life.

4. Preserved salted radish

Tangy and extremely salty, preserved radish is usually sold chopped and diced in packets, available at most Asian supermarkets. An opened packet usually keeps for 1–2 weeks, although it is best to refrigerate immediately after opening in hot and humid climates.

5. Prawn (shrimp) paste

Prawn paste has a pungent odour that belies its ability to add to the array of special, subtle flavours that make Thai cusine unique. Either a light pink with grayish hues or a dark, purple-brown colour, prawn paste is available in most Asian supermarkets. Made from tiny fermented prawns known as *keuy*, it is an ubiquitous ingredient in many Thai dishes, whether as part of the cooking process or as a condiment.

6. Thai tom yum paste

Spicy and tangy, tom yum paste can liven up the flavour of meat and vegetable stir-fries. It also gives Tom Yum Prawns (see page 87) an extra punch of spiciness, should one prefer it that way.

7. Betel leaves

Betel leaves are known for their medicinal properties, such as curing toothaches, headaches and indigestion. Traditionally, betel leaves are chewed with the areca nut, which acts as a stimulant.

8. Chinese celery

Chinese celery is widely used in soups and stir-fried dishes to add flavour with its aromatic, pungent taste.

9. Galangal

Galangal is a rhizome belonging to the same family as ginger. Its colour ranges from ivory to pale yellow, with pink-tinged tips at the ends of its bulbous stems. Galangal is privileged in Thai cooking over its better-known cousin the ginger, adding a sharp and refreshing zing to soups and curries.

10. Hairy basil leaves

Easily distinguishable through fine hairs covering its stem and leaves, hairy basil has a similar taste to Thai basil.

11. Hot basil leaves

Hot basil or holy basil, as it is otherwise known, has a strong peppery taste, with a hint of mint. Many Thai dishes employ its use in generous proportions to add spice and flavour. Hot basil can be recognised through its dark purple stems and rounded, jagged leaves.

12. Kaffir lime leaves

Easily recognisable by their dual leaves shape, kaffir lime leaves are used lavishly in Thai cooking. Even when used sparingly, kaffir lime leaves impart a flavour that cannot easily be replicated by any other citrus leaf substitute. It is available in fresh and dried form in most Asian supermarkets.

13. Lemon grass

Lemon grass is a highly aromatic herb with long, slender leaves and bulbous stems. The stems contain glands that release pungent oils when sliced or bruised, which impart a distinctive, lemony flavour to Thai dishes.

14. Chinese keys

Chinese keys or *krachai* packs a far stronger punch and flavour as compared to galangal, having an intensely gingery and pungent taste. It has long, slender roots that resemble fingers, attached to a knobby root. Chinese keys is preferred for its use in seafood dishes.

15. Sawtooth coriander

Although very different in appearance, sawtooth coriander is a variant of coriander (cilantro), and has a similar taste and aroma, only stronger. It has long, sword-like leaves that are covered with fine hairs.

16. Screwpine *(pandan)* leaves

A highly versatile plant, screwpine leaves are used for more than merely wrapping food. They lend a wonderful aroma and subtle floral flavour to steamed rice, meat dishes and desserts. Fresh screwpine leaves should be a dark, shiny-green colour, with a stiff spine.

17. Pickled garlic

Pickled garlic is sold in jars at most Asian supermarkets. Pickled garlic has a crunchy texture with a reduced garlicky flavour and sweet and salty undertones.

18. Tapioca

This root vegetable is often sliced and deep-fried into chips, which serve as a popular snack in some Asian countries, or used in desserts such as puddings and jelly. It is available in most Asian supermarkets.

19. Thai basil leaves

Thai or sweet basil is the most common variety of basil used in Thai dishes and other world cuisines. It has a sweet, peppery aroma, faint purplish stems and provides a subtle taste not unlike anise.

20. Bird's eye chillies

Small in size but extremely fiery in flavour, bird's eye chillies feature as a popular ingredient in Thai soups, curries, salads and stir-fries.

21. Green mango

Sour, tangy flavours are favoured in Thai cooking, which is why green mangoes are commonly employed in salads, or consumed as a snack in itself combined with salt and chilli. Choose green mangoes that are blemish free, with a sharp, fresh scent.

22. Kaffir lime

Kaffir lime is easily distinguishable by its coarse, bumpy skin and dark green colour. Although the fruit is not commonly used as an ingredient in Thai dishes, grated kaffir lime zest provides a subtle and refreshing flavour, fragrance and colour as a garnish.

23. Green peppercorns

Green peppercorns are the unripe berries of an evergreen vine. Green peppercorns retain the original colour of their unripe stage by drying or through pickling in brine. Fresh green peppercorns are widely used in Thai cuisine, adding a sharp, fresh flavour. However, they tend to decay quickly if not preserved or dried.

24. Pomelo

Pomelos have a thick, spongy rind and sweet, juicy flesh. The rind can be used in flavouring soups, or made into preserved candies. A ripe pomelo is usually pale green in colour.

25. Tamarind pulp

Tamarind is characterised by its dark brown, moist, sticky flesh. Its sweet-sourish taste is a common feature in many Thai dishes. Tamarind is available in its pod, or in blocks.

26. Water chestnuts

Native to China, water chestnuts have a thin, dark brown papery skin and crunchy cream-coloured flesh. Water chestnuts can be used in sweet and savoury preparations.

weights and measures

Quantities for this book are given in Metric, Imperial and American (spoon) measures. Standard spoon and cup measurements used are: 1 tsp = 5 ml, 1 Tbsp = 15 ml, 1 cup = 250 ml. All measures are level unless otherwise stated.

LIQUID AND VOLUME MEASURES

Metric	Imperial	American
5 ml	$1/6$ fl oz	1 teaspoon
10 ml	$1/3$ fl oz	1 dessertspoon
15 ml	$1/2$ fl oz	1 tablespoon
60 ml	2 fl oz	$1/4$ cup (4 tablespoons)
85 ml	$2^{1}/2$ fl oz	$1/3$ cup
90 ml	3 fl oz	$3/8$ cup (6 tablespoons)
125 ml	4 fl oz	$1/2$ cup
180 ml	6 fl oz	$3/4$ cup
250 ml	8 fl oz	1 cup
300 ml	10 fl oz ($1/2$ pint)	$1^{1}/4$ cups
375 ml	12 fl oz	$1^{1}/2$ cups
435 ml	14 fl oz	$1^{3}/4$ cups
500 ml	16 fl oz	2 cups
625 ml	20 fl oz (1 pint)	$2^{1}/2$ cups
750 ml	24 fl oz ($1^{1}/5$ pints)	3 cups
1 litre	32 fl oz ($1^{3}/5$ pints)	4 cups
1.25 litres	40 fl oz (2 pints)	5 cups
1.5 litres	48 fl oz ($2^{2}/5$ pints)	6 cups
2.5 litres	80 fl oz (4 pints)	10 cups

DRY MEASURES

Metric	Imperial
30 grams	1 ounce
45 grams	$1^{1}/2$ ounces
55 grams	2 ounces
70 grams	$2^{1}/2$ ounces
85 grams	3 ounces
100 grams	$3^{1}/2$ ounces
110 grams	4 ounces
125 grams	$4^{1}/2$ ounces
140 grams	5 ounces
280 grams	10 ounces
450 grams	16 ounces (1 pound)
500 grams	1 pound, $1^{1}/2$ ounces
700 grams	$1^{1}/2$ pounds
800 grams	$1^{3}/4$ pounds
1 kilogram	2 pounds, 3 ounces
1.5 kilograms	3 pounds, $4^{1}/2$ ounces
2 kilograms	4 pounds, 6 ounces

OVEN TEMPERATURE

	°C	°F	Gas Regulo
Very slow	120	250	1
Slow	150	300	2
Moderately slow	160	325	3
Moderate	180	350	4
Moderately hot	190/200	370/400	5/6
Hot	210/220	410/440	6/7
Very hot	230	450	8
Super hot	250/290	475/550	9/10

LENGTH

Metric	Imperial
0.5 cm	$1/4$ inch
1 cm	$1/2$ inch
1.5 cm	$3/4$ inch
2.5 cm	1 inch

index